BODIES OF WATER

To Allan
from Sarah

BODIES OF WATER

SARAH
LINDSAY

1986

Unicorn Press, Inc.   Greensboro, N. C.

Poems which have been or will be published in *Asylum,
A Carolina Literary Companion, The Chester H. Jones Foundation
Anthology 1984, Heartland,* and *loblolly* are reprinted with permission.

Library of Congress Cataloguing-in-Publication Data:

Lindsay, Sarah, 1958-
   Bodies of water.

   I. Title.
PS3562.I51192B63   1986   811'.54   85-28948
ISBN 0-87775-186-2

Unicorn Press, Inc.
P.O. Box 3307
Greensboro, N.C.   27402

TABLE OF CONTENTS

Forsythia teeth of the sun pop
from leafless whips willowfingering
a soggy wrapper
sloughed from a crisp winter—
Fool yellow before green, tweet color
shrill sings in a burst at the first nudge—
touch waiting right in the skin to be touched

WAKING

That bump in the night like steps running
        faster without coming closer or escaping
        is your heartbeat
That one like a gavel calling order
        or a hammer making wood stay
        is the boots of a thief downstairs
That one like your heart
        imitating sanity but fading
        is the clock stolen, going away
That one is Leonardo's funny man
        doing over and over and over cartwheels
        cartwheels in a square

Morning she is the in and out soft sound
        reminding you how to breathe,
        slow and easy, just by wanting to,
        a trick you'll never master since it's a trick to you—
        you'll never fall calmly as daylight
        or wake without thirst and a full bladder—
Morning offers ways to find a way.
        Drop the splayed little man, flapping
        his four arms four legs, on a slice of cork in water;
        this is a compass. Spinning he learns to swim.
        Floating he is a paper flower, and blooms.
        To first fill the bowl
        take her firmly by the ankles
        till her head dips
        or yours
        this is a divining rod, says water, water, water.

WASHING DISHES IN THE NUDE

Up to my shell-pink nose in dogwood, cottonwood,
every blooming thing that huffs its seeds
of prickle into the air, and shielded
by screens that let in wasps but not a breeze,
while red shinnies up the thermometer and my sink
of dishes threatens to breed:
can't stand the heat, can't leave the kitchen.

Feet stick to the floor, an unparticular grease,
grit, film laid by cooking down the ages. Slick warm trickle,
armpit, juice glass, dishcloth squeak poked in,
suds squashed out. Itches dictate
though nails are occupied—I leave bubble scraps
on mine, satisfied.

                    Meat blood, thickened oil,
the unique slime of new egg, the crust of fried.
Lettuce shriveled, grape juice reduced to glue,
flour paste, crumbs, old yogurt blooming green.
How else are the good things made, but with
sweet sticky sand and powder, slime and slurp, drops
on the floor, dirty dishes, dirty dishes?
Slaps of cold water rinse us, and I shine,
hear the key, wait to tell him what he knows,
the best cooking takes a mess, and silly ingredients.

POSSIBLY THE MOST ENJOYABLE
PHASE OF THE ROMANCE

As usual, after plenty of warning,
abruptly—but I didn't catch the time—
my heart cracked open and my head fell in.

You boring heart, laced with old glue.
You stupid head, wallowing in wet red oxygen
like a cherry cordial.

Shall I offer this man too
a broken terra cotta pot
holding a softened apple?
(They look. They shake. The fruit
bobbles around, or bounces and rolls away.
Or they drop it. But sooner or later
we don't know what comes next.)

These last nights alone I rock,
I thread a banana and quilt together
my furniture, windows, body,
books, food, songs, imaginary beasts,
with sweet awkward mushy stitches, in case
he ever asks to be smothered.

THE HOUSE I LIVE WITH

Windows scoop sun through the walls
of the honeycomb built and born with me.
Some rooms sparkle like ginger ale
with old dust rising, some the wind cleans.
I can hopscotch the patterned rugs
with my eyes shut; the screen door's
twang and bark were my first words.
The grass is full of clover. If brick teeth
loosen in various mouths, if
bats borrow the attic and sometimes squirrels
cork the gutters—almost anything
can be repaired or survived.
But ivy lays against my house so many
three-fingered hands, like hands
of children trapped in faery tales.
When I come near sleep
half of me is out with them looking in,
with bottomless eyes and tiny breakable bodies.

BOWL OF CUT GLASS

Between my hips and arms I carry
pain in a punch bowl
filled full as leaves room for more—
red juice,
that sticky liquid jello Mom made for sick stomachs,
blood that pricks out abrasions, noses cuts—
bowl of cut glass, heavy as a wedding bell,
broad as a sea full of chariots,
lapping when I move
like someone tonguing her lips before she speaks—
smells like vinegar, the clear red dye
round an Easter egg in a cup,
like Marat's bath full of medicine
and salt. I can
look in and see the face
of my face, full of hollows between my hands
and wobbling. I can
vanish my hand in to the wrist
and bring it out whole.
No place to pour a river of gasoline
with its flame tied to the end, no
grass wanting red dye, no way
to gush without staining me from the heart down.
I try bearing it like well water,
learn a little grace.
Hold it for the slow drinks of the sun.

NGC 5128: GALACTIC COLLISION IN CYGNUS

The swan is pure swan, doesn't know it,
doesn't know it flies, almost forever,
in our line of sight. From another planet
they may see a leopard, lizard, goat,
another swan. From here we say
galactic collision in Cygnus, meaning
a swan flies between us and the tidal distortions
between two systems. But each whirling dish
of stars is so much emptiness
nothing crashes. No two suns flame together
like racing cars. Two fields swing
in airless silence and tear each other's gases
from spiral to shambles. Superheated,
scattered, left so impoverished
they will make in themselves no more stars.

Our bodies are made of dead stars' hearts,
scientists say. Maybe some of us instead
are wads of gas untimely ripped from twisting
darkness in spiral arms. Maybe
the galaxies we used to be still limp through space
without us, through swans, leopards, lizards, goats.
No more boomeranging on curved wings, popping new lights.

If I want to fly now I'll need a scope
that takes me to the swan's back, gives me distance
so full of zeros everything is small. Scattered,
impoverished—I wonder if you tore forever too,
when I reached and your fingers passed like air through mine.

GEODE DISGUISED AS BOWL OF WATER

Newpenny brick wall behind green coins of leaves,
chalk parking lot sliced with yellow, a smooth sky,
zagged by the chain of a power saw's moan eating wood.
A goldfish dropped in this day, I drink it,
wide-eyed but unsurprised, the gills of my mind
beating and blinking. But a goldfish bowl
can break; one waltz step of a blown curtain
has cracked afternoons to the heart.
All this translucence disguises a plain round stone
that a breeze can split. A cool breath rises
from the halves, packed like a pomegranate
with the crystal and darkness of a buried year.

TURNING

Spiral is the trail that comes closer by going away.
    Water falling down drains, liquid ascent of iron rail
        above wedges of stairs, tripping the inside foot's steeper climb,
            spirals. Microladder of twirled rungs coiling our little genes
          spirals, turns back, so the words stutter enough to make flesh.
A mind open-lidded to morning strings it to yesterday mornings,
at night plays another string; the pitch of a June or Christmas
    rings a shiver in sister seasons, while days between are still.
        Fall through your time like a needle through yellow curtains;
            memory thread gathers, tugs sweet Midsummer Eves in a bunch
        between wrinkles of days, or picks out kisses from dullness.
    Climb the twisted ladder, blind feet groping down one, down.
I find you out of everyone, our Fridays pulled tight together
    and snagged to my Fridays since: you, water I couldn't hold,
        handrest and stumble, backbone and reason of my splitting cells,
          summer, Christmas, bright needle, closer by going away.

BODIES OF WATER

Given the ratio of our solids to water
we ought to be puddles with a skin of slime;
in a bathtub ninety-nine percent of me
doesn't know whether it's in or out.
The universe is empty as we are wet,
matter a contamination fantastically rare—
on intergalactic markets we're gold.
Squiggles and corkscrews hold us together,
sugars and salts, our freakishness composed
chiefly of the enemies iron and oxygen,
but making do with any impurity—
chlorophyll, lithium, anger, chocolate, love—
that dropped in water makes rings.

THE STUDY OF FOSSILS

Coelacanth
eyes are deep as the ocean,
caves of something flickering and fixed like time.
With bulldog jaw the coelacanth shovels water,
with chunks of fin shoves water buried under water,
sea fresh and old from lapping crusts and rubbing itself
down where the coelacanth
once hid without trying, kept secrets unknowing,
grew bones on a pattern old as dry oceans,
mentioned in stones,
and barged on, a museum unaware,
a body worth feeding.

In a net dropped for something else
a coelacanth dies of fighting.
In another net, another, dead,
bashed and shredded, dented, dripping scales.

They are too ugly to arc from polished board
over a whiskygold hearth,
too strangely named to slap in batter,
awkward celebrities—
breastless, untalkative, unlikely
to piss on Carson's desk.
Pets should not have such teeth.

The scientist tastes the blood of his lip
after months of straining water
as the coelacanth in his net
batters itself past help.
He struggles it into the bright blue shallows
for the last and only live photographs.
He must learn how ancient fins were moved—
back and forth? in circles?—must look
past the mouth hanging open, filled with light water,
and eyes, of a color where no man swims.

INVENTOR OF THE DELTA WING

There should be a ghost here. The driveway is long, narrow, overgrown,
the house hides in trees, mushrooms vanish and reappear in tangles
beyond the garden. At night everything is blacker than the sky and where is
his spirit that widowed her? that drew half the world's air into one lung
years after the other half expelled him? He made them regret it, breathing
over his basement tables, his fingers his eyes the finest pencils graphing
wings, sharp wings, clever to fly over water, fast as the quiver of strings
when he stopped work for her and the lute. Fast as she ran down stairs once,
fast as he was gone. In the house a tiny gray lady, a ghost-white dog
just as tall, fool, car-chaser, garden-crasher, thief of whole goudas
and shortcakes. No haunting, unless the curled tip of one string, snapped
from the lute's elbow on the wall, is moving in a mothwing breeze.

PERMISSION TO ENTER THE CAVES

My mother is going to Altamira
Permission to enter the caves arrived
    in strange words under strange bright stamps
Her best travel books may now prove true,
    and the faded red one where the girl raised her candle
    and ran to her father afraid,
    and was famous

My mother is going to Altamira
She stands before the mirror, her lips in parentheses,
    stroking with her tube of American Rose—
    presses her mouth shut, takes a print
    on one scented square of tissue
She will make a print kissing me goodbye
She sprays mist of plastic smell on her hair
The caves will be damp, so deep,
    perhaps with a far-off drip,
    insistent as the faucet
    she reminds me to keep tight

My mother is going to Altamira
She has knitted my father a vest of crimson yarn
    to cover his chest in the coolness under the sun,
    where the painters wore deerskin, torchskin,
    mixed pigments in their palms
Paprika and pepper she smears on the fat of pork roast,
    warning me I'll learn to cook now,
    tuning the oven's blue flame that pinks her face

My mother is going to Altamira
The good grades in Spanish her dad required now bloom for her,
    the degree my father and I in turn interrupted
Her passport photo smiles like a high school senior
She has a new plaid suit with thin brights of red
    and a pair of shoes that might walk to the earth's core

My mother is going to Altamira to see the scarlet bulls

EVERYTHING HALF PRICE

He laughs at the rattle I dig from a box
of lipsticks and magnifiers. It's coated like everything here
with dust, fly specks, ink or elderly light.
Anyway your niece is too old, he says,
and entertains me with battery-powered back-scratchers,
a miniature gold pineapple for roaches.
A cushion perfect for my back, no tag:
My mother used it here, the owner says, in black;
You understand. I nod like the crouching dogs
on the next shelf. Go poke soft wads of yarn.
With a goat-head shoehorn he points to books—
Toby Tyler, weight loss—and stationery for closed colleges.
He fills my fingers with rings, gothic globs of metal
and stained glass, cameos of the homely, and brushes them off.
There are chains to hang glasses on the chest,
sweaters over shoulders, pencils on lapels. Yards of pearls.
He wants the bust they drape: A girl
all white and smooth, hair molded with a ribbon,
a white blush on her cheek, lips turned toward shoulder.
He bids with the owner in black. That's what he wants.
The secret under my belly is heavy as marble, but will never
learn to be so still, so permanently sweet,
never learn that portrait smile, a mouth that needs nothing.

BUBBLE BATH

Ease skin slow into smooth sweet water, hot clinging
all over pink flush, lily of the valley fills lines
in palms of feet and hands
Bubble skins snap cool on the edges of soft stone body,
pink blue lights inside
Slide down lily to collarbone bubbles nape bubbles,
belly island with navel puddle, toes wiggling coral,
fingers float
Valley of the porcelain tub, steam, moist face,
lie white lambskin in bubble wool
To be clean, babywrinkled, squeaky bleached—
loll and wallow, read the ceiling, swish warmth uncurling
through weakening water
Bubbles tick open uncounted, careful as sleep's breathing,
cleaning the head through
Upheave swash slop shakykneed into cool air, drop drop
lascivious notes on foamless draining water, gulp, unbalanced
heft over the edge
Mirror mist shows no shape of the thing all clever curves
cups to catch dirt

NIGHT WALK

A nail on the wall opens wings and flies.
The last stair stumps my leg——a bar of shadow;
the spider, a freckle, won't run off my knee.
On the sidewalk pitted with stones or holes,
lizard shadows twist from scraps of branches,
the wood fibrous, white chicken. One piece
wears filthy feathers for bark, a dead beak open.
Above it the seventeenth moon on a pole,
strung to a block of moons,
shrinking to burrs with white electric needles.
Above that, stars glide flashing red and green.
Pale white ones on the edge of sight
vanish in the dark center of the eye.
Only air to walk through, when
thick thread breaks clinging across my knees.

BRINGING HEAVEN DOWN

Past ripening the spring day begins to fall.
In a haze of their own atmosphere
girls play a casual softball,
their cries mixing with pollen,
new drivers on streets gutter-wet from washed cars
clear the throats of their tires on corners.
The sky is blue, unluminous;
the sun is gone, the moon full, posed clouds
gray and white. — A sky that imitates
the thick tempera of painters
trying to bring heaven down
to rooms of aristocrats. It hangs
low as these gilded ceilings
over the cars, the basemen,
for the heavy feet of gods
to punch through, as they fall from paintings,
blowsy and foreshortened in their absurd pursuits.

BONE HORSE

Charcoal lines speak, like darkness,
in a thick tongue,
shadow is their whisper.
Roughness grows fur, an eye
deepens fierce as a horn,
a stick man thins
like smoke rasped over stone.

The little bone horse,
half his slender face younger than half,
runs faster with broken legs
that never touch ground—
his feet long gone, his body still,
unmade tail flying on wind.

PAS SEUL

At first he looks less mad than when he danced.
Panther black no longer slants his eyes,
now softly ringed like any tired man's.
His dark clothes barely touch him, so they hide
the dappling shadows of his ribs and flanks;
the muscles that stirred such trouble when strung tight
do little more, some days, than lift his plate
of untouched food, in a gesture that feeds light.
He may hold motionless as no one can
through endless afternoons, stage-bright and blank,
or count invisible petals in one hand,
or pace for hours, then pause
watching the room's high window,
barely still on the tips of the soles of his feet.

EATING LETTUCE IN PUBLIC

Inside your shoes you are stuck to your socks,
trying to wiggle your skin free, when the waitress
arrives, her apron white as the notepad
for listing your sins. She places your salad
beside the ice water. (The glass, sweated to the table,
awaits overfull your first attempt to drink.)
With hollow black olives the salad stares at you,
stiff as art—hunks of purple
that blue the egg bits, crumbled meat
kissing jellied tomato hearts, onion geometry,
all on lettuce swatches big as your hand.
In moments you are cowlike,
a pale green frill at your mouth;
you know, almost, that on your nose
stands one cream drop of dressing
with its contrasting speck of pepper.
There is a mirror behind you. The knives,
spoons, glasses, shaker tops all twist you
with your vegetable garland, glinting.
Diners look carefully elsewhere.
Do not touch your nose, or reach
for croutons in your lap.
Nothing is proven against you.
When the eating is over each of us pays
in the last room, with no one to laugh.
Dressing drops endured may tilt the scale
where your sheepish heart is weighed against a salad,
lifting your sins to heaven, lighter than lettuce,
as you cry in the clean cloth napkin over your face
in defense, then wonder, I am pure, I am pure.

DIRECTIONS TO MY HOUSE

You are lost again or you wouldn't be reading this.
Face whatever your back is turned on and walk.
Take the right rights and whatever is left.
Pass a food store, a school, and several minor accidents.
On the street whose name you know so well the sign looks wrong,
go by a bird bath, a dead squirrel, a bridge over mud,
a lamp post smeared "I love," a glacier's boulder.
Now pick the house that isn't too big, whose windows
turn red at sunrise, whose lawn holds a place
like a cupped hand for three white violets.
This one should fit your keyholes.

Try the mailbox. Real letters should be brought
on a silver tray. The newspaper, you'll find,
fits neatly in the trough
made in the grass by rain and a drunken tire.
As you bring in the good stuff, check the two-foot maple
for birds' nests.

                    Now the stepping stones.
Slipping stones, really, all of them lettered in mud:
Don't forget, Careful, Go back for it,
Hurry, Relax, Change your mind, Go directly to jail. . .
At the door, the cowardly lion-head knocker
and deep gilt bell: Ignore them, come in.
If you smell sweetness, run to the kitchen,
take from the oven and eat. If the parlor is dusty,
let the dust hide it. If the TV is talking,
put the cloth over its cage. If a book is out of place,
read it. If the dog kicks in her sleep, run after her.
If the window is full of gray strangeness, take this hall—
first on the left if you're thirsty, but quick now—
open the door of the quietest, livest room, softly,
find in the blankets a box of dazed flesh.
That's me. Us. Get back in, it's morning.

Sarah Lindsay designed *Bodies of Water,* hand-set it
in 12 pt Perpetua type, printed it on acid-free 70 #
Warren's Olde Style with a Vandercook SP15 hand
press, sewed it, and bound it in Hopper Skytone and
Beckett Buckeye. She wishes to thank Teo Savory
and Alan Brilliant, and dedicate this book to
Granny Tennessee.